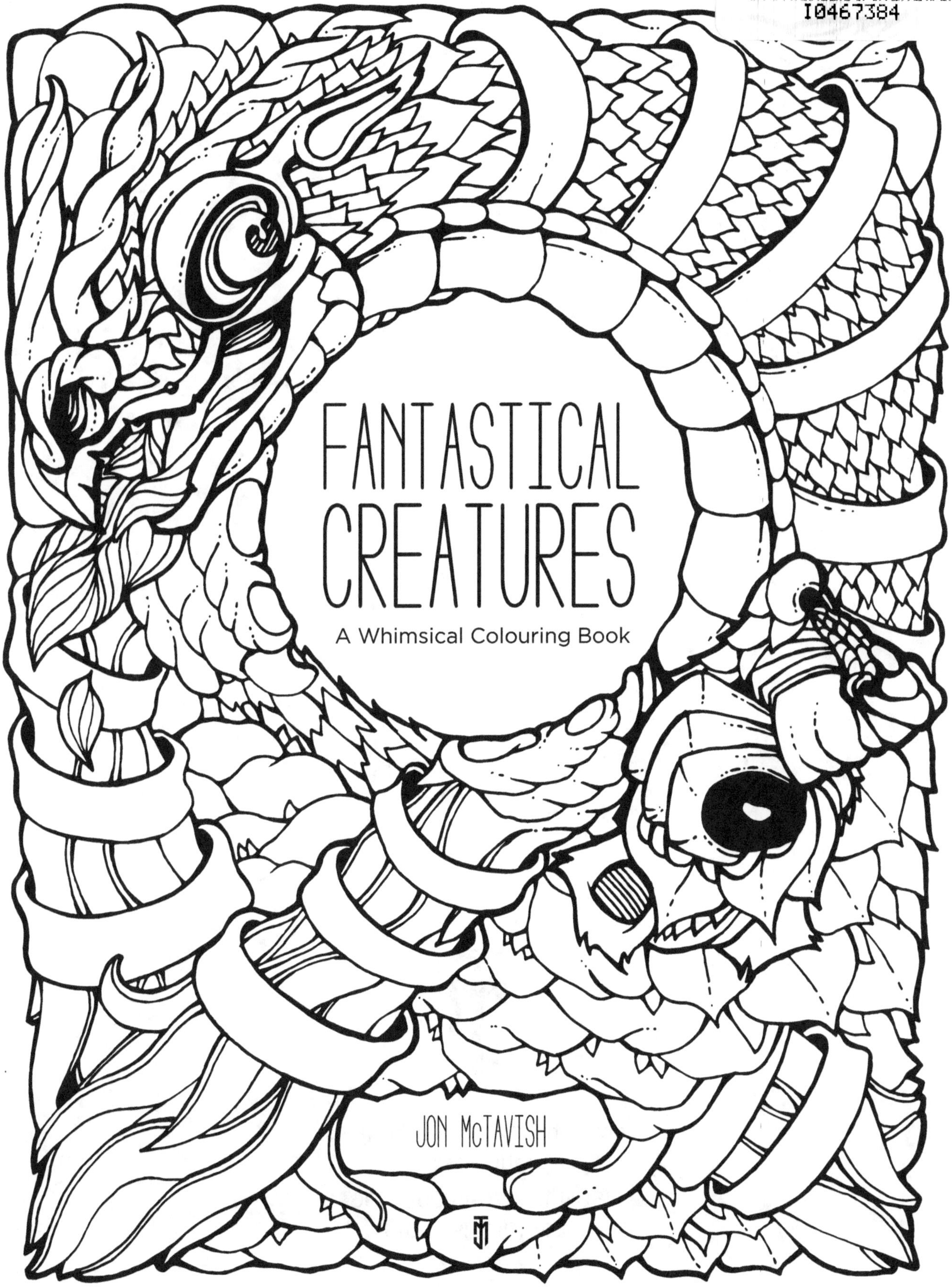
FANTASTICAL
CREATURES
A Whimsical Colouring Book
JON McTAVISH

ISBN-13: 978-1519600196
ISBN-10: 1519600194

Share your colouring.

#FantasticalCreatures
@FantasticalCreatures

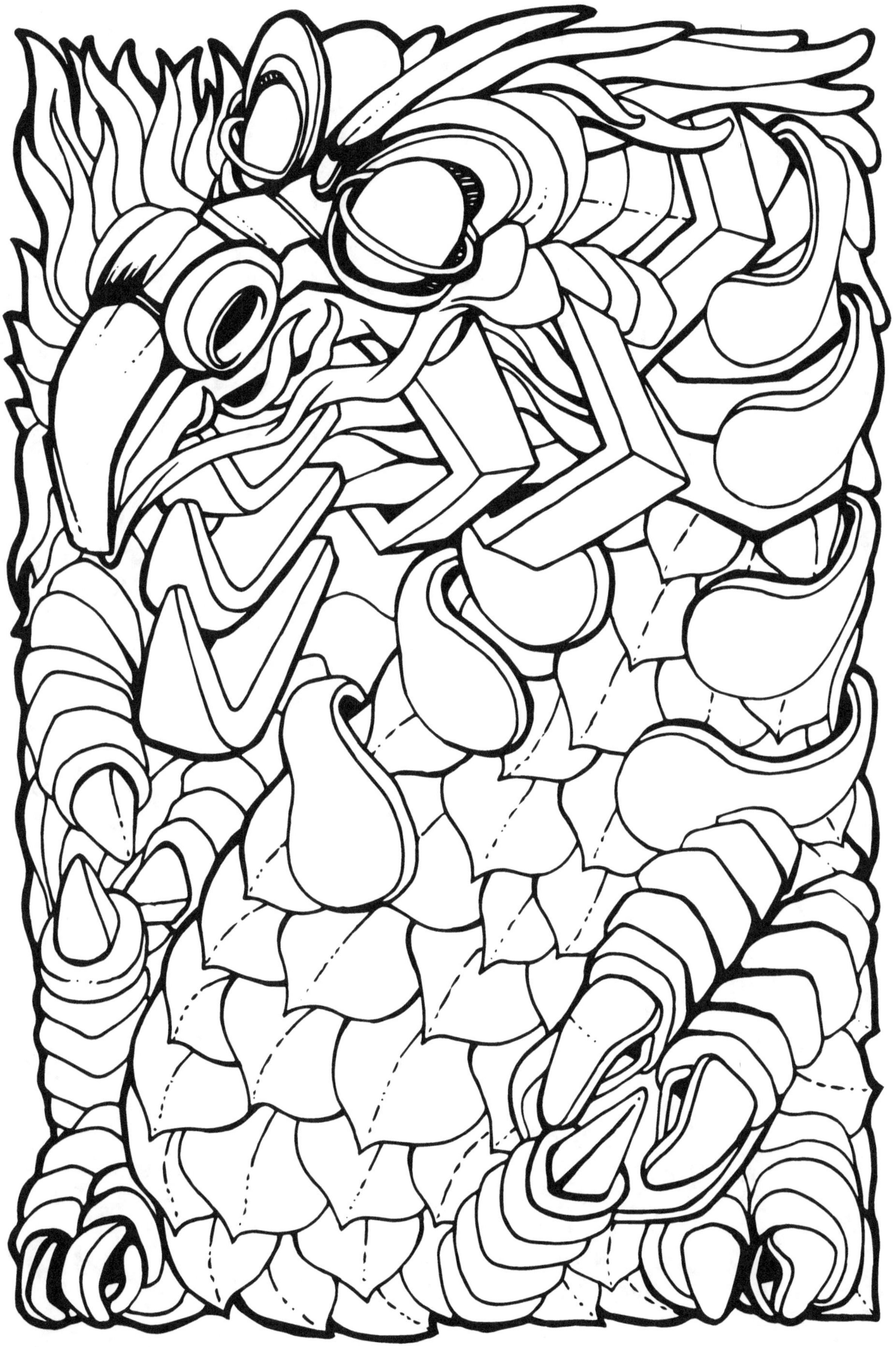

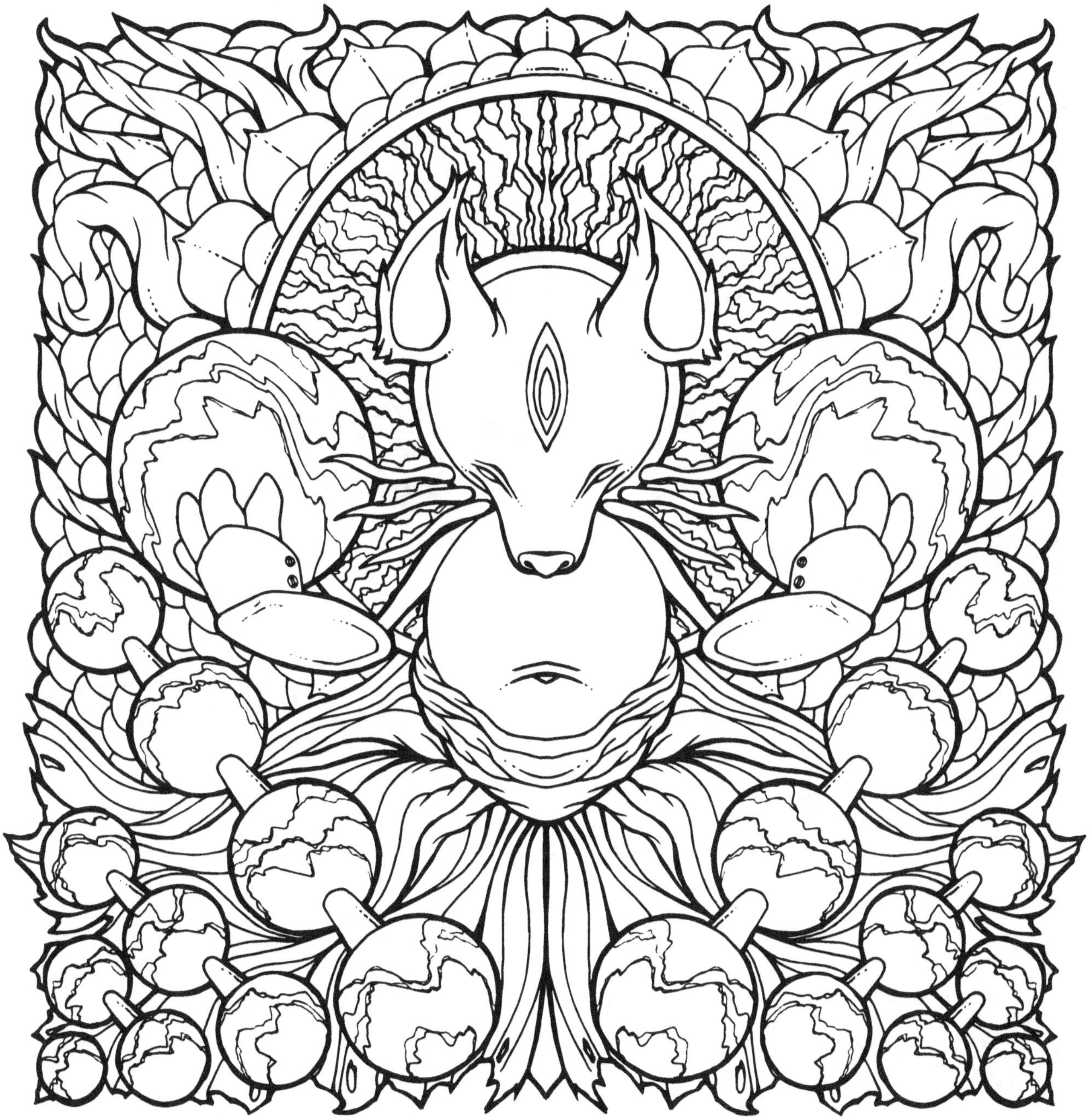

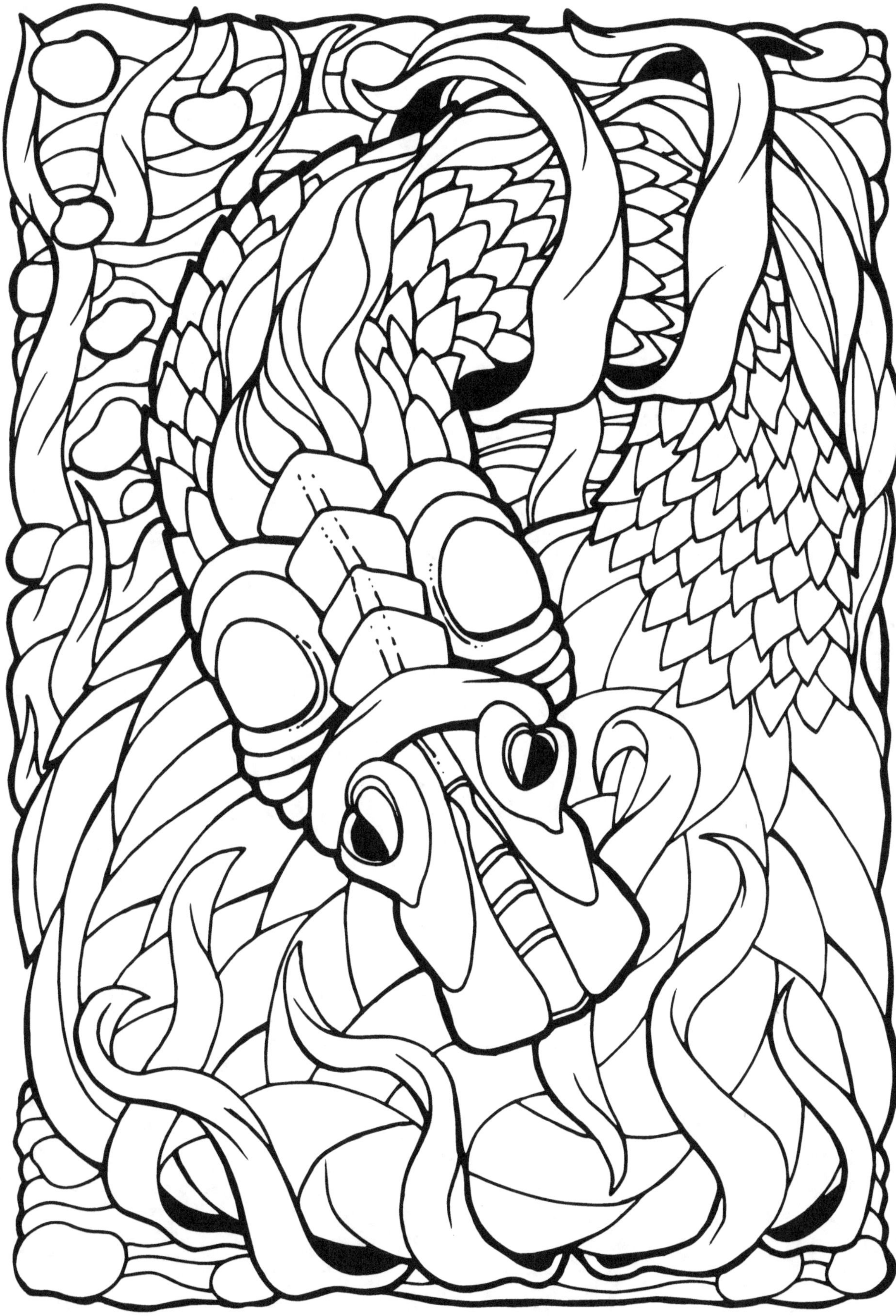

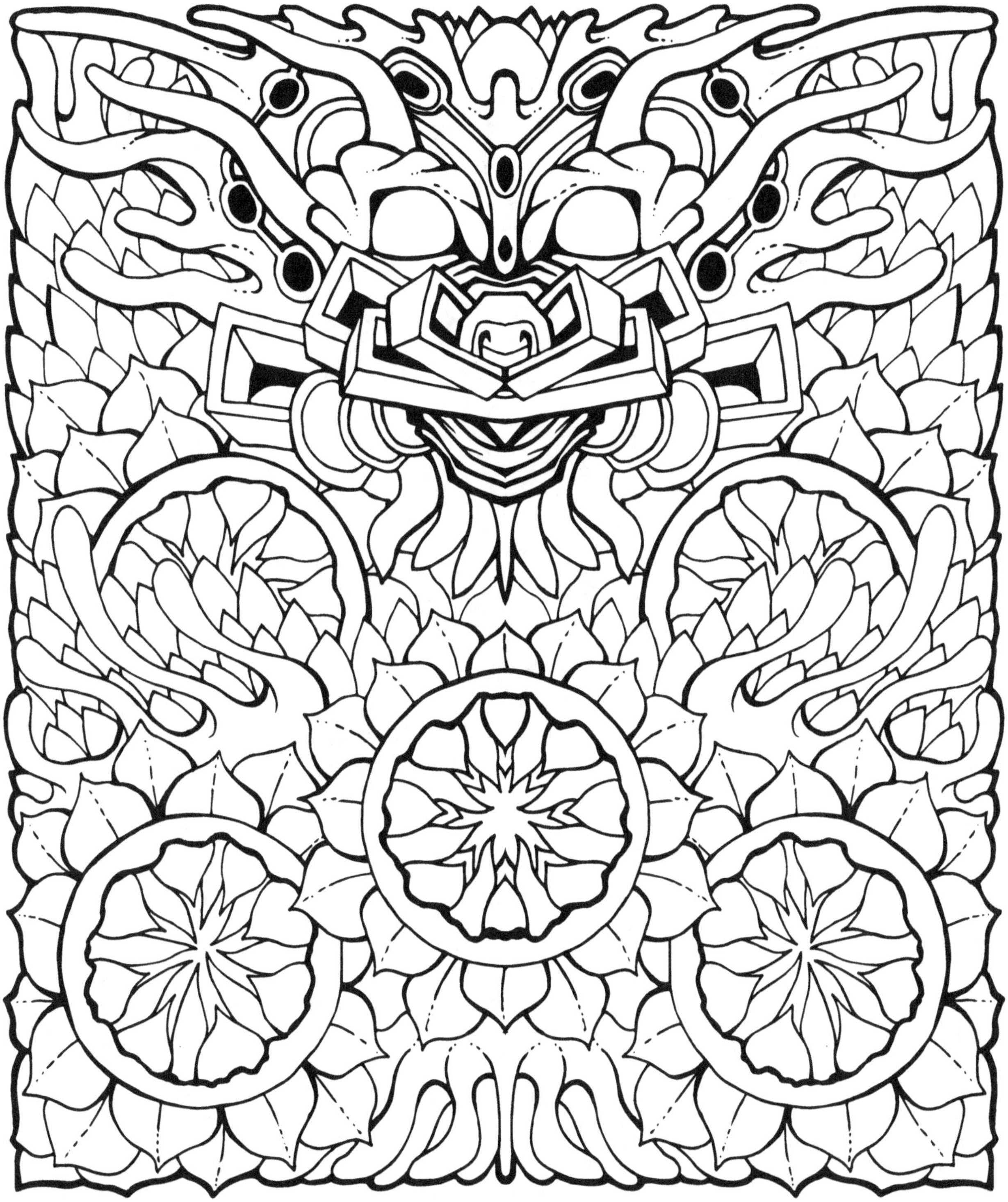

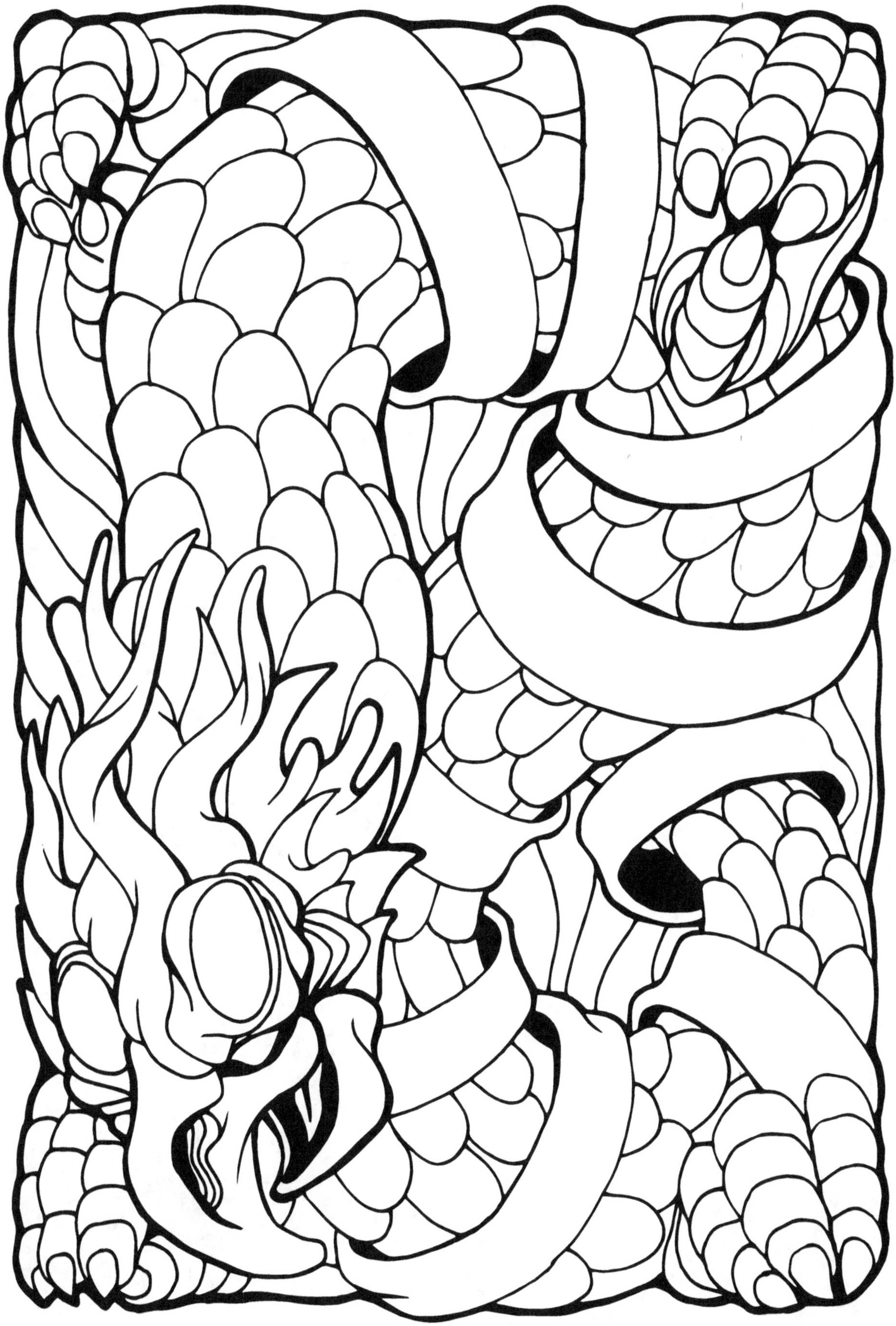

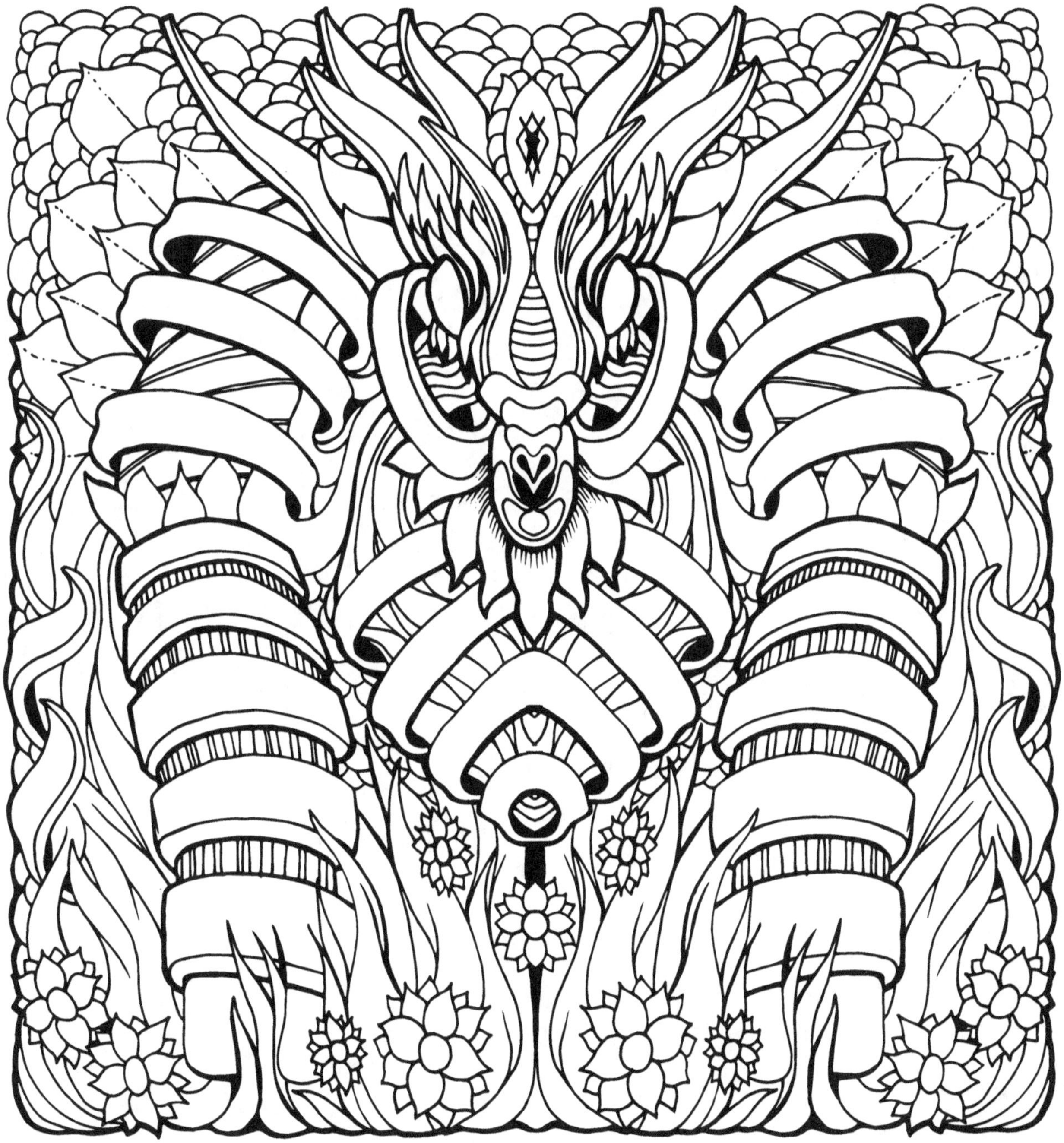

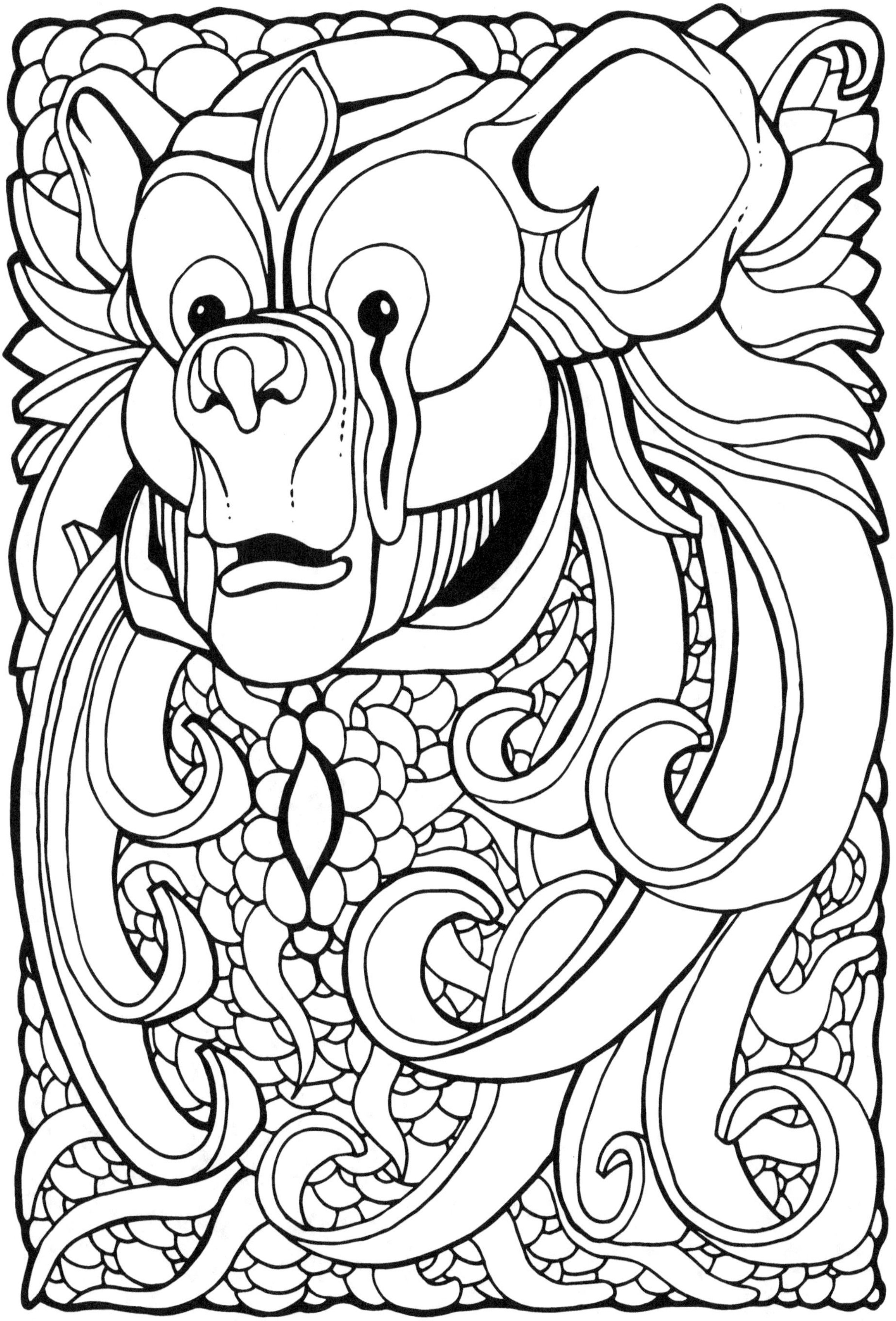

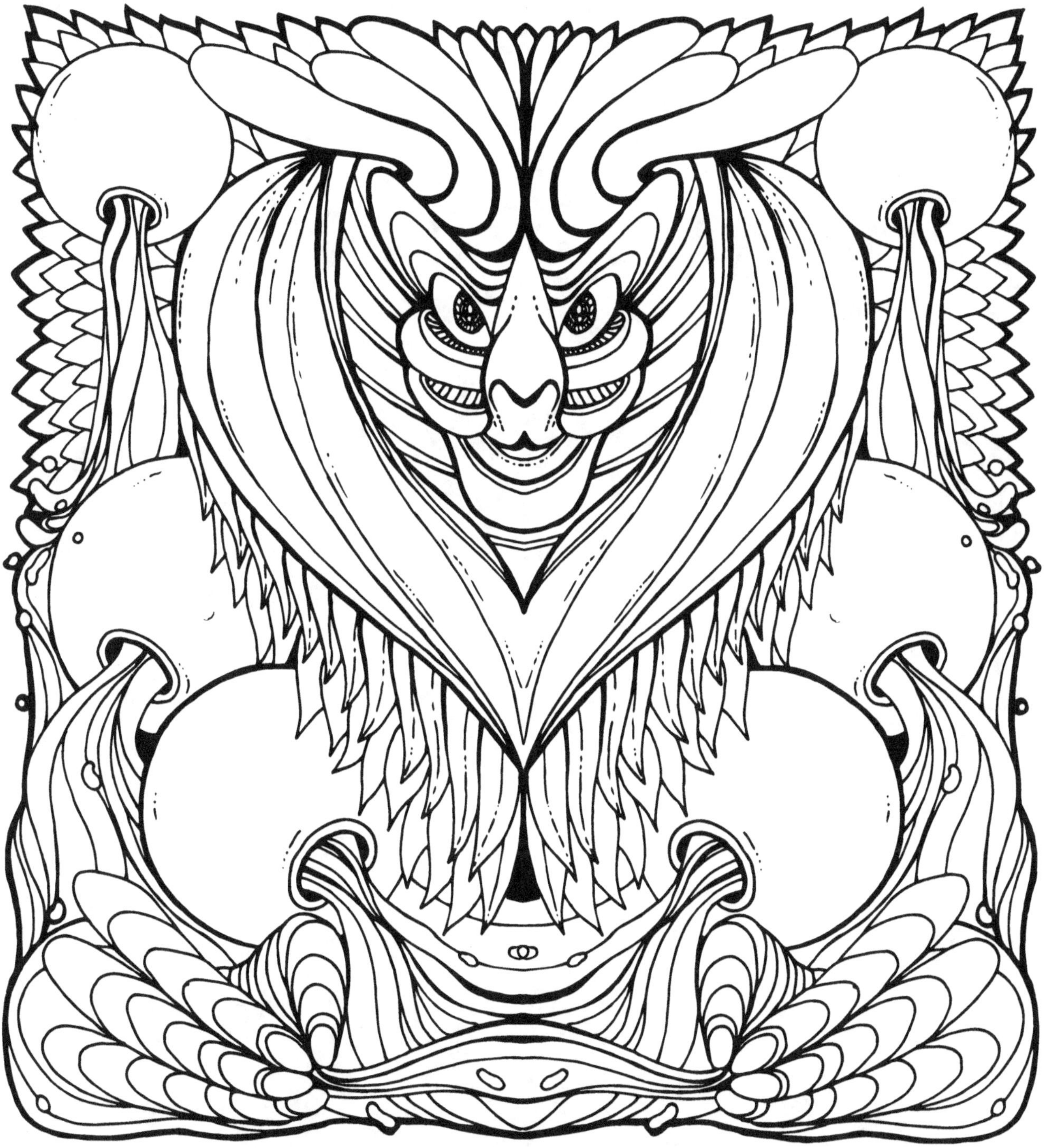

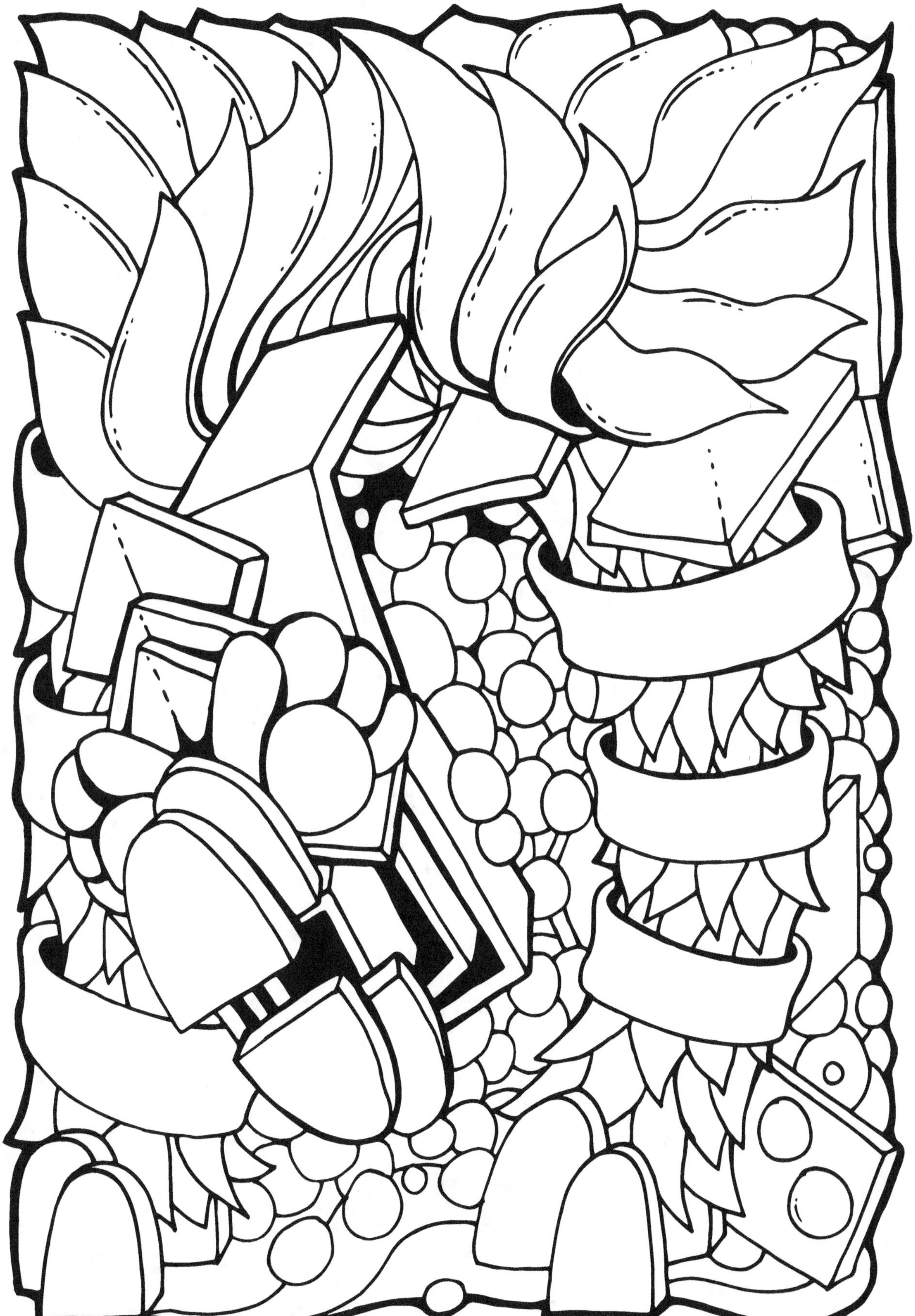

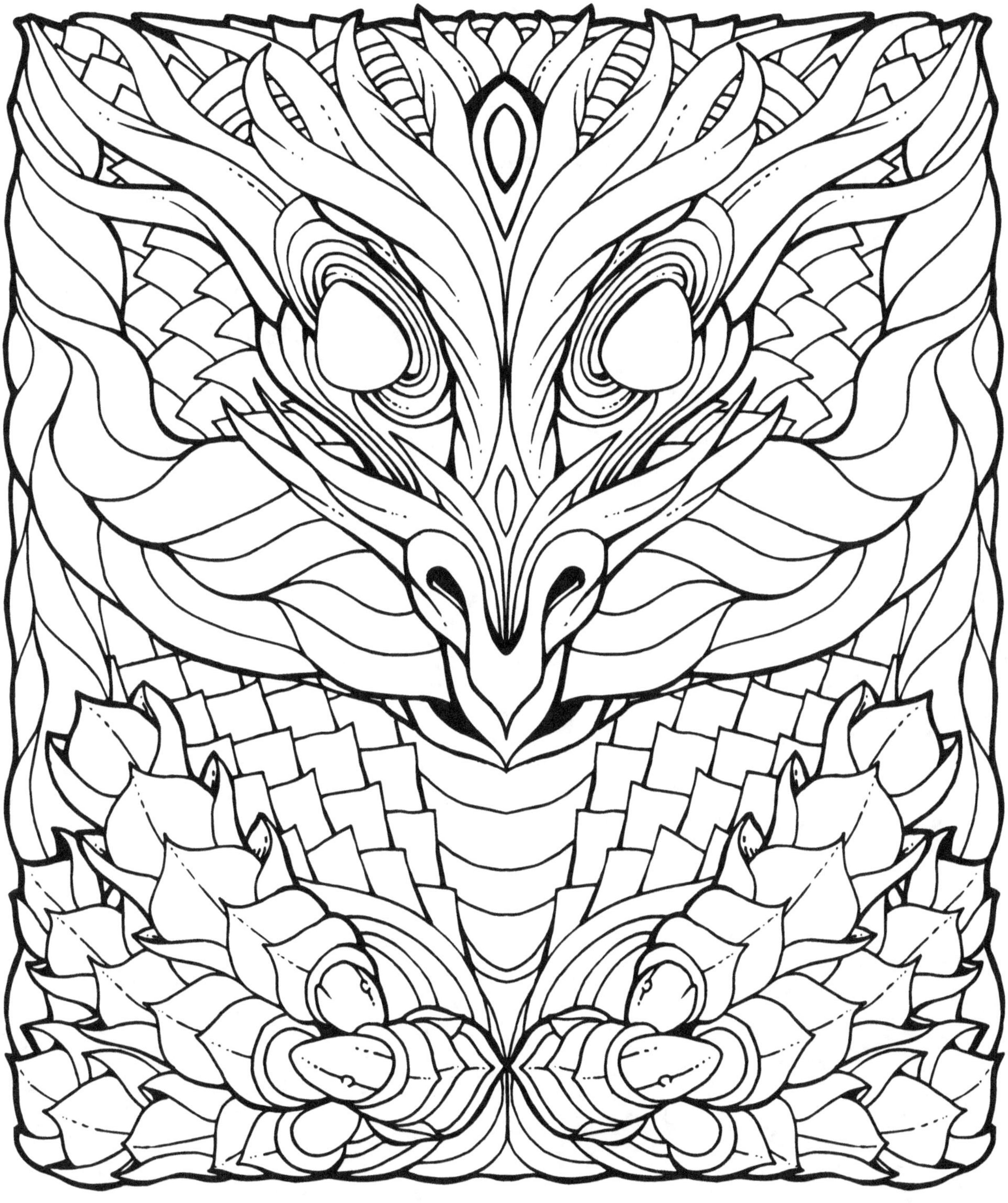

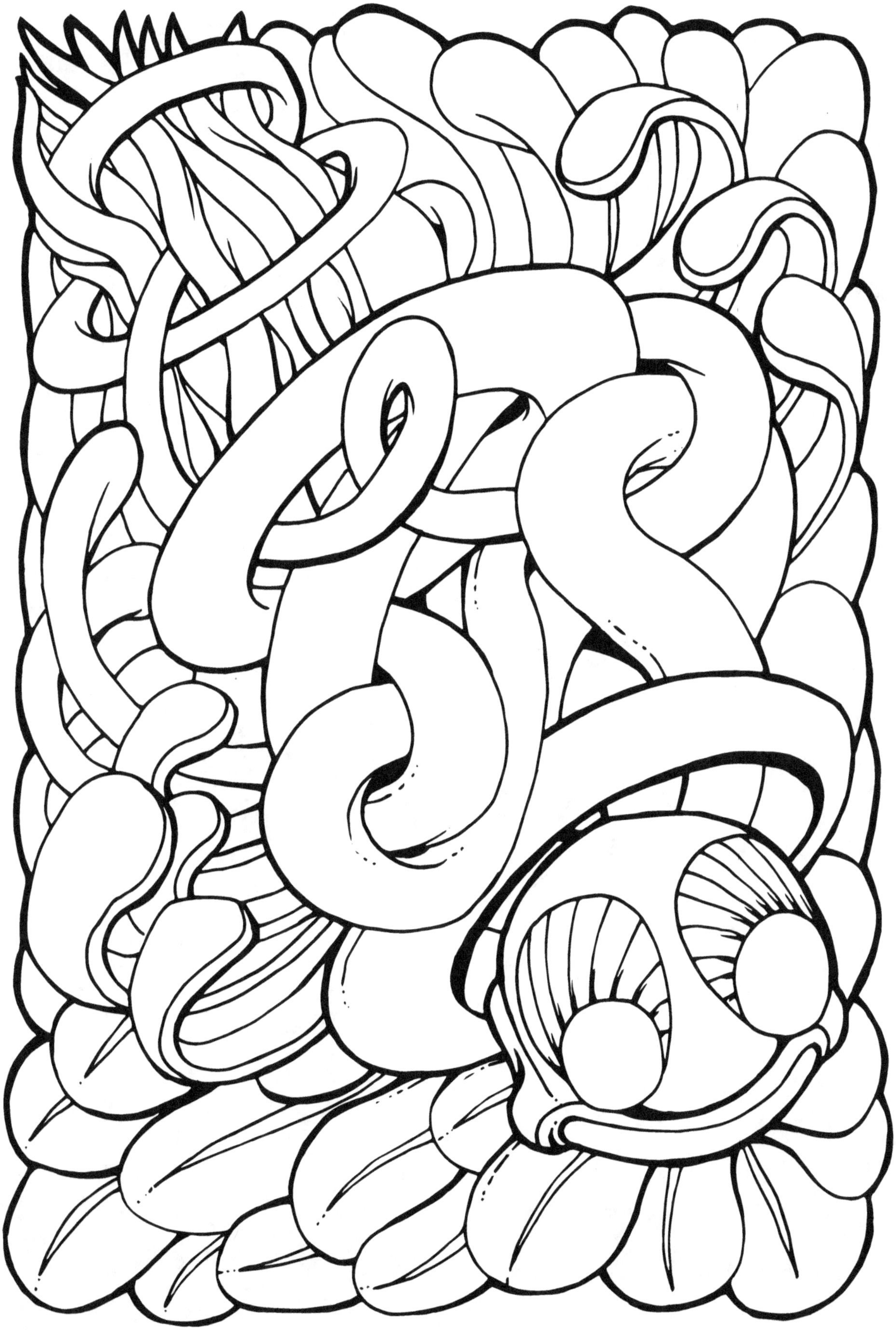

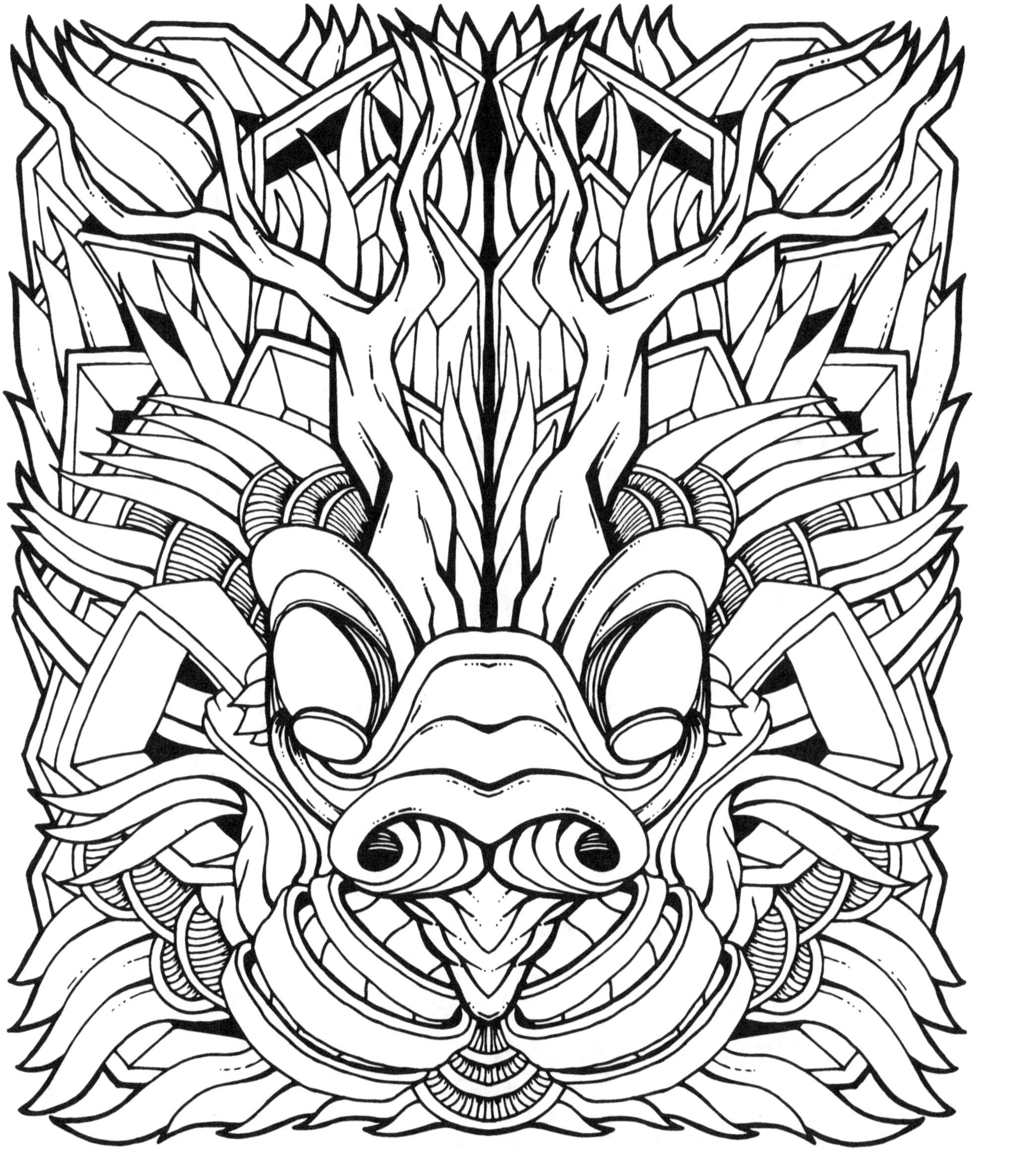

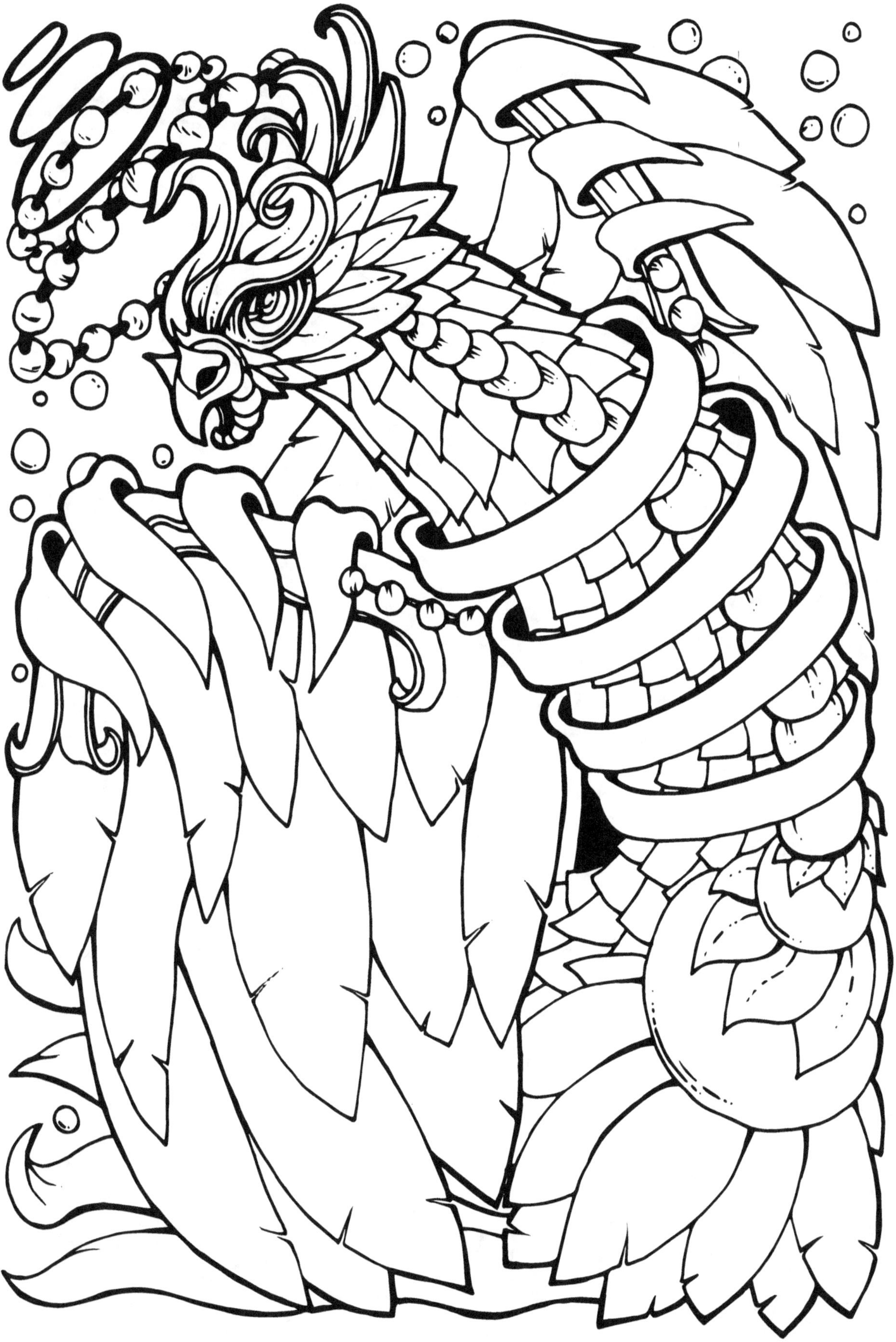

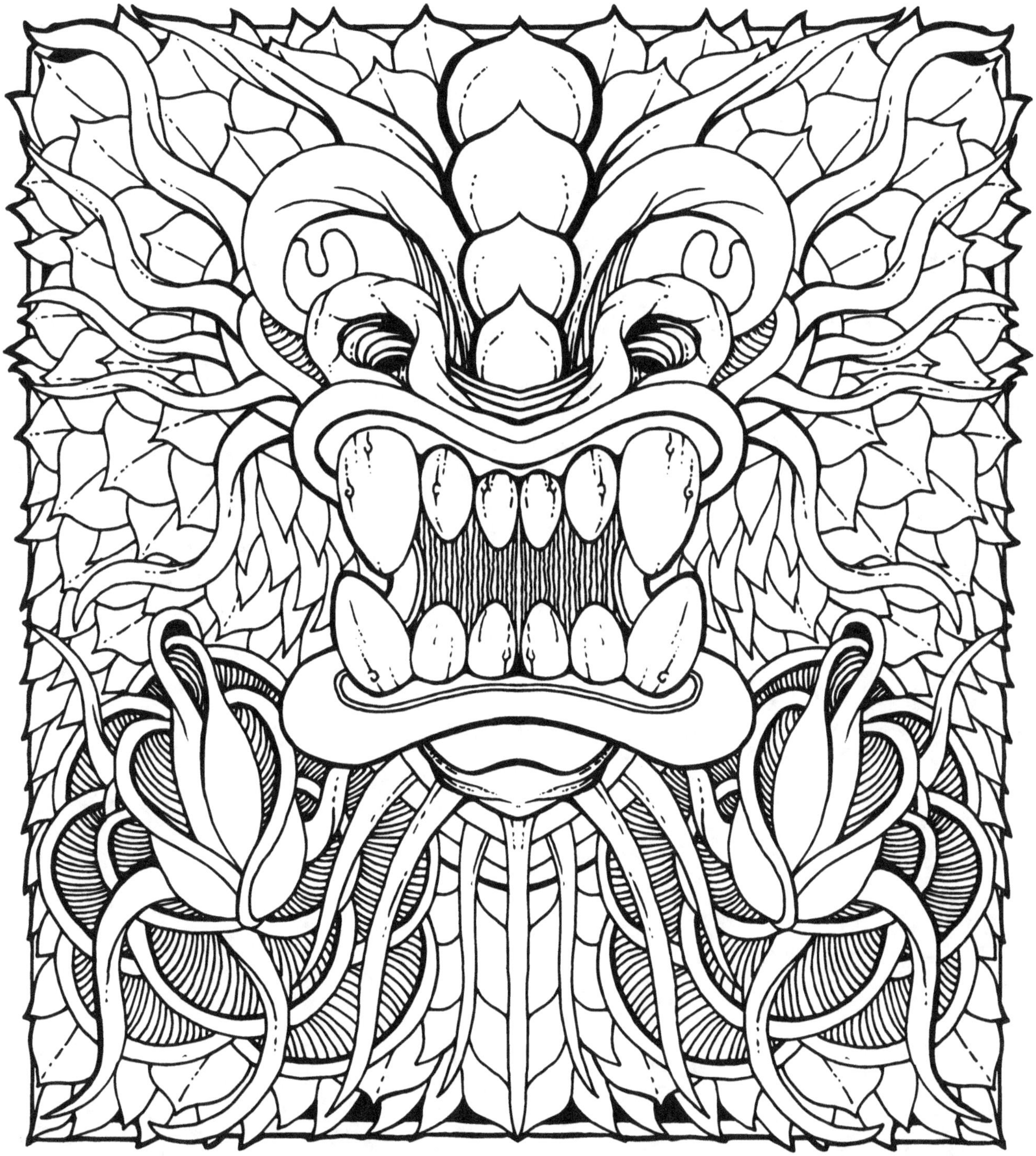

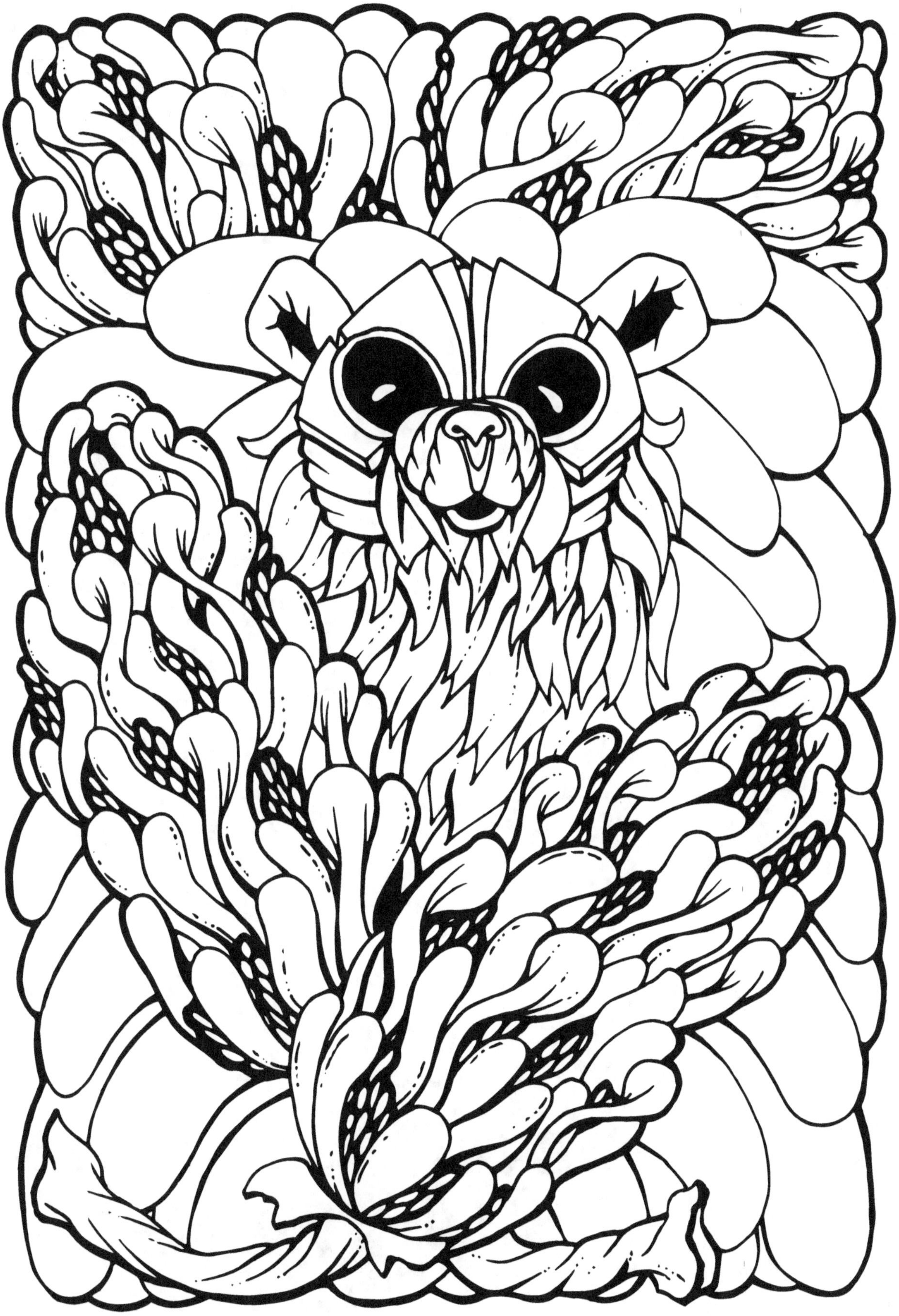

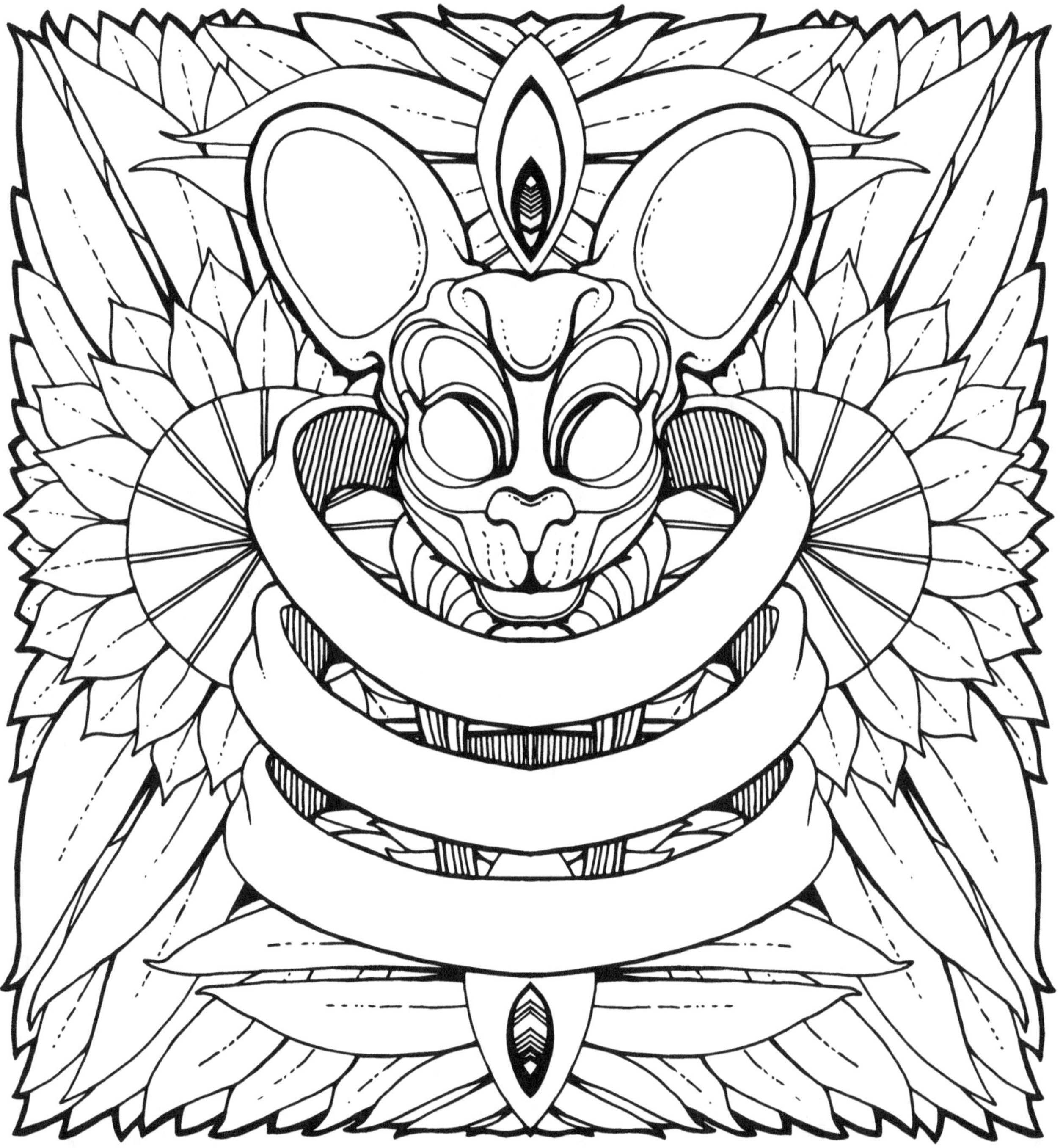

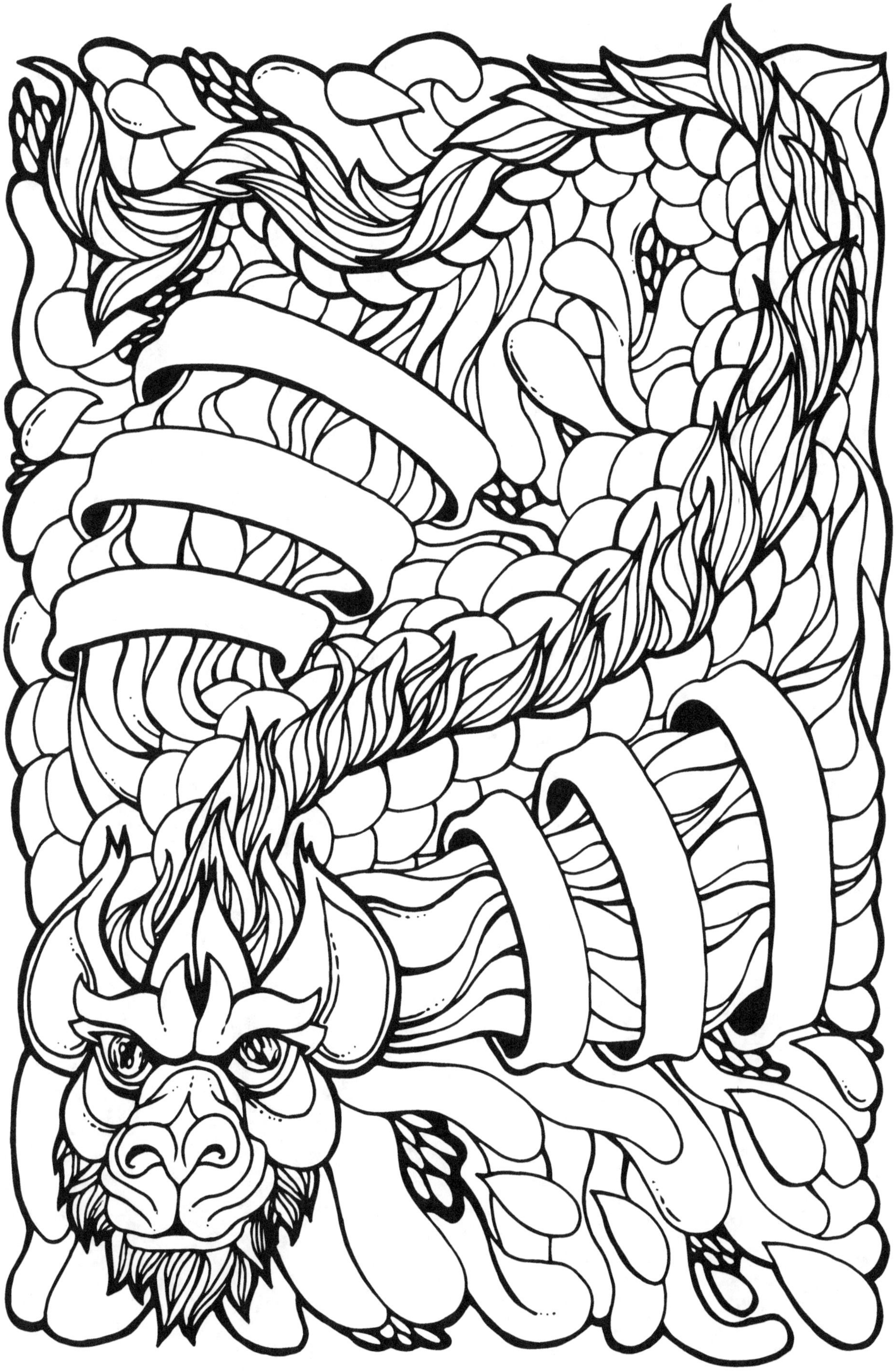

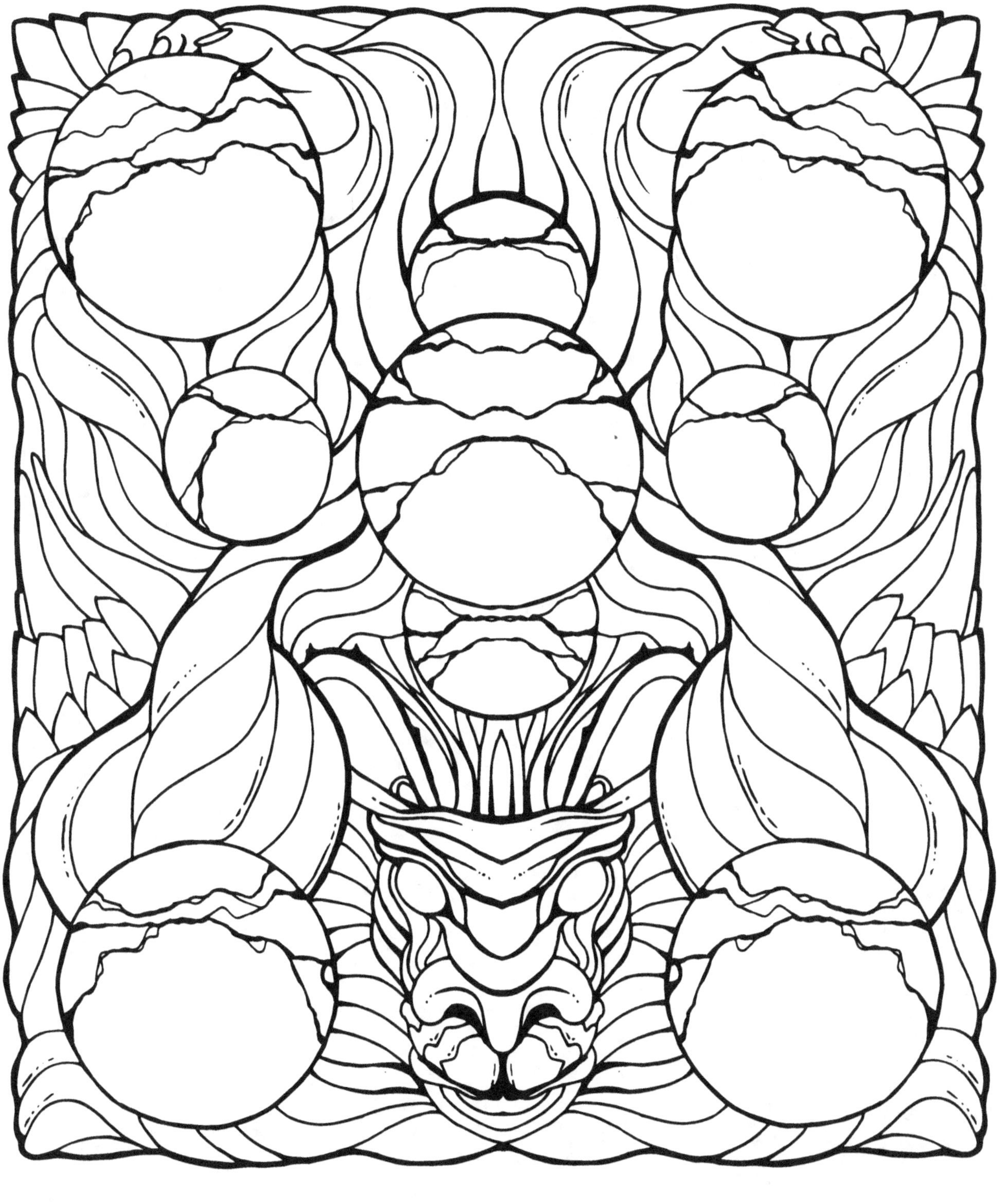

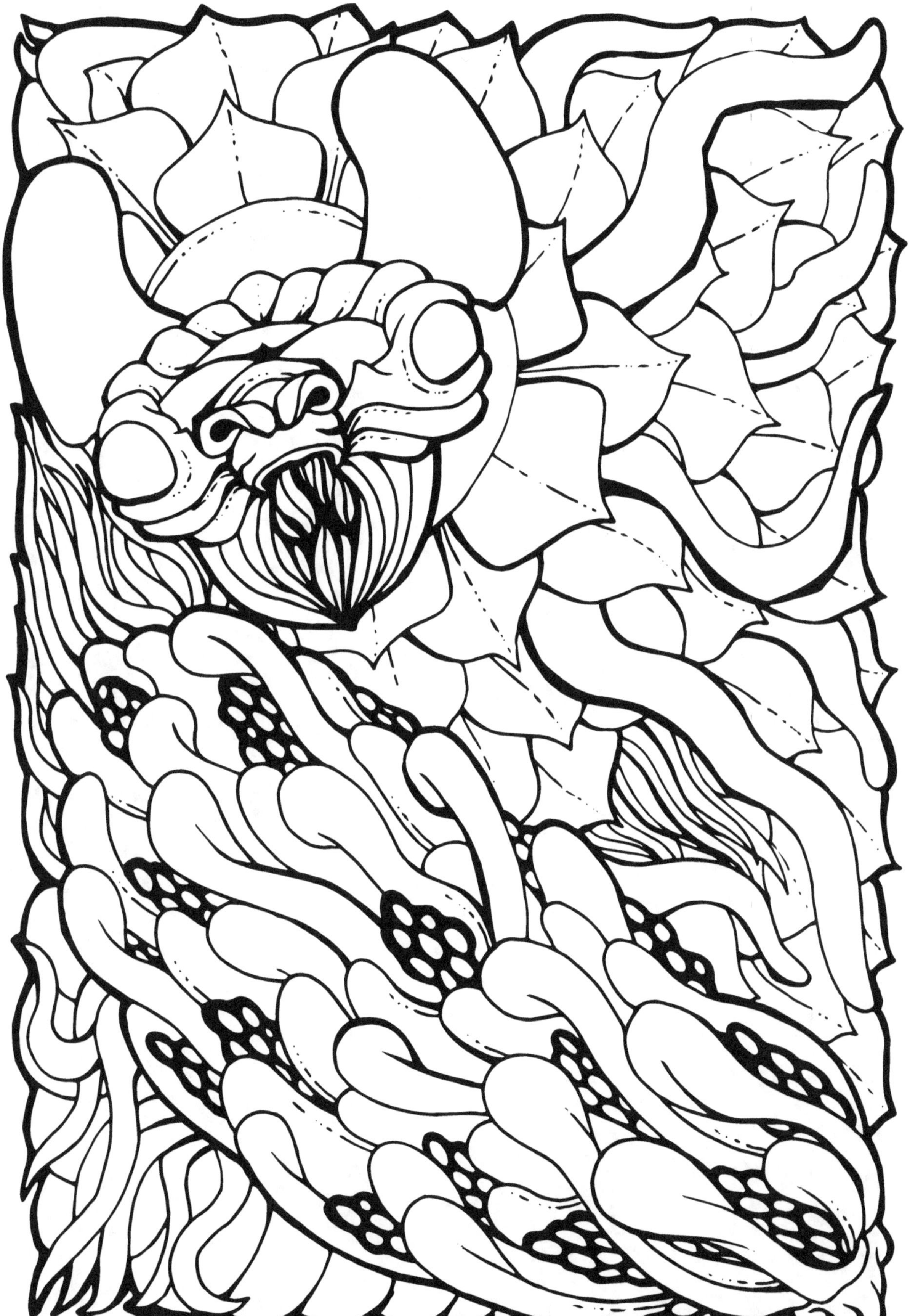

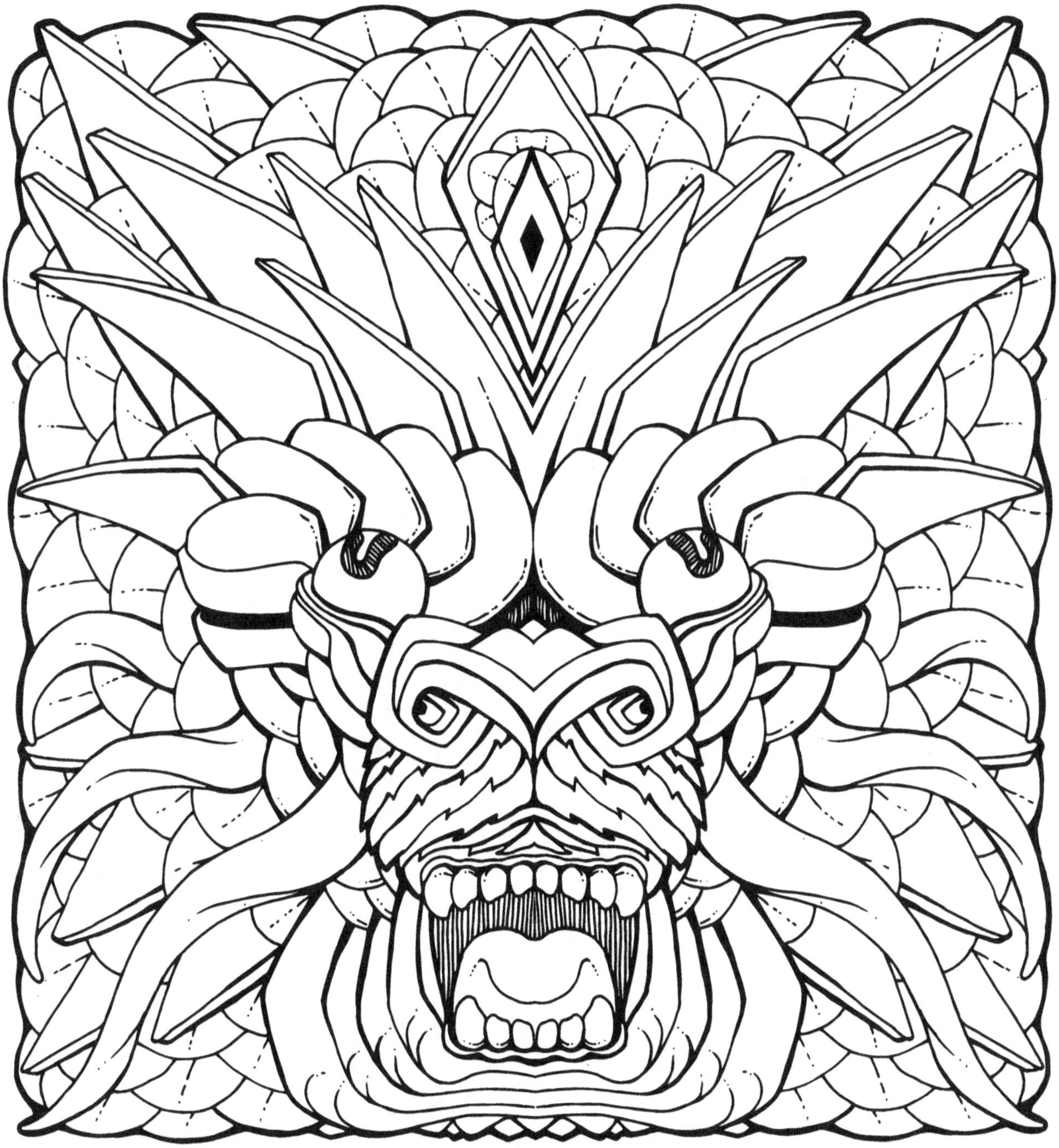

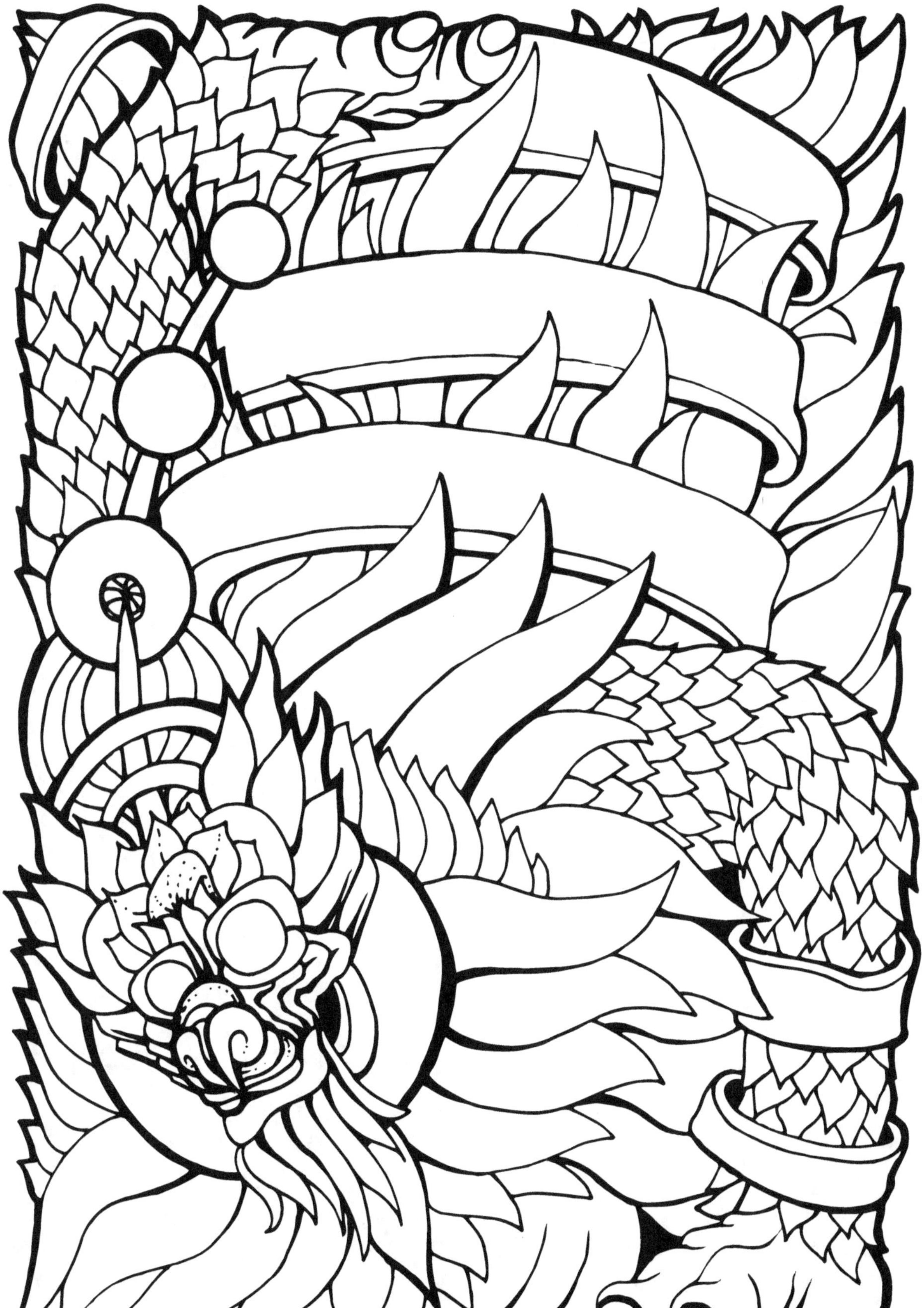

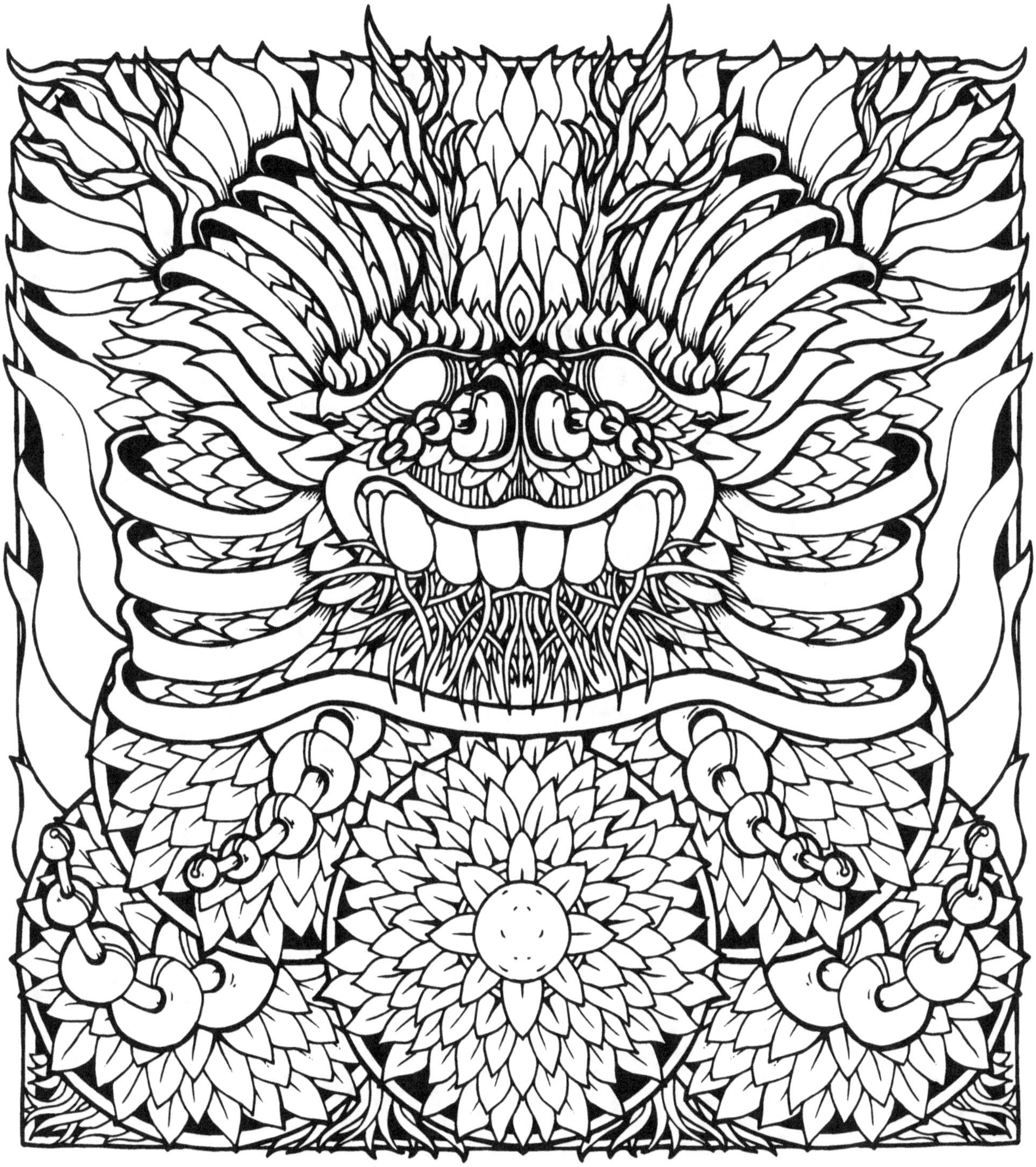

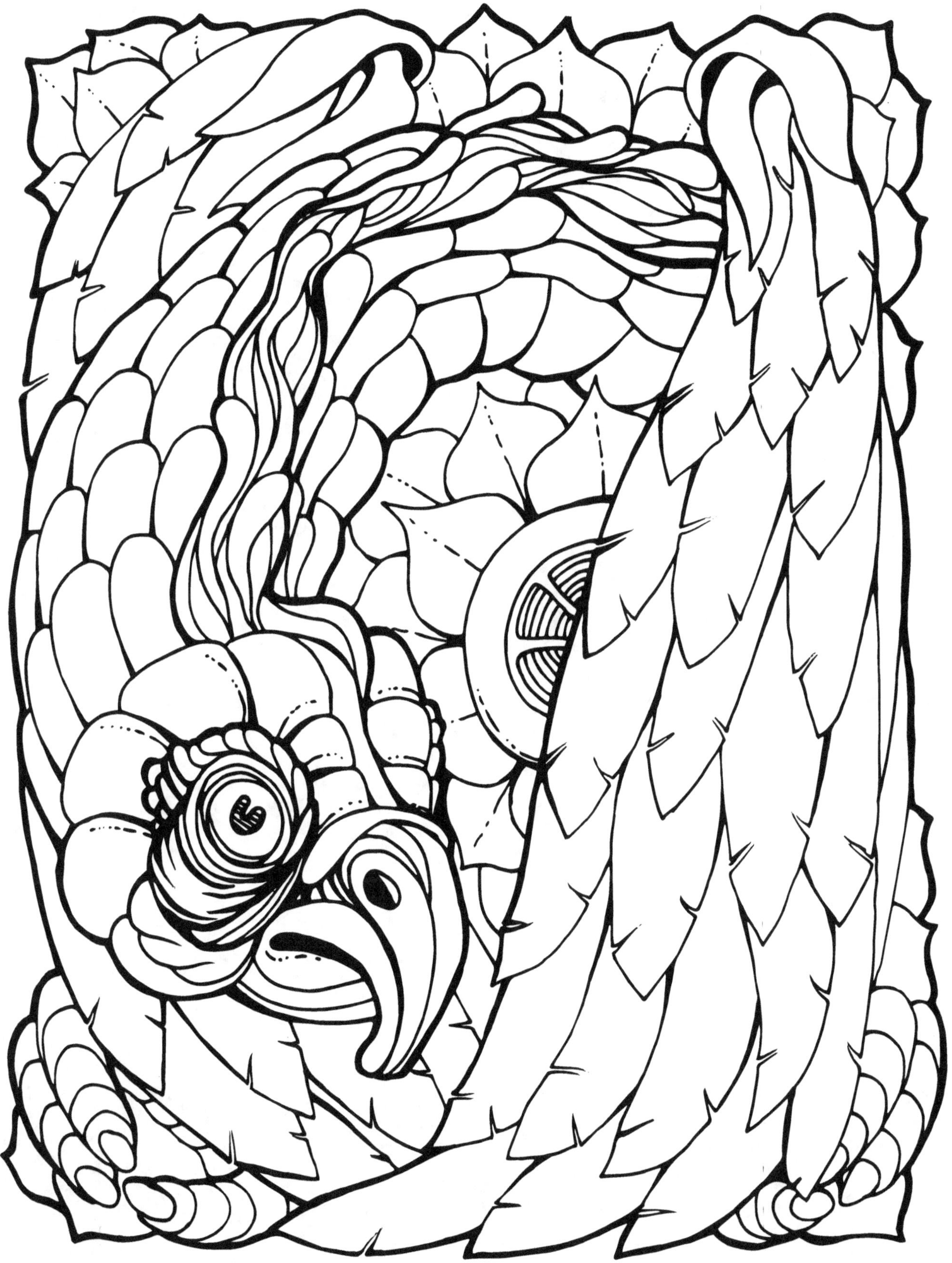

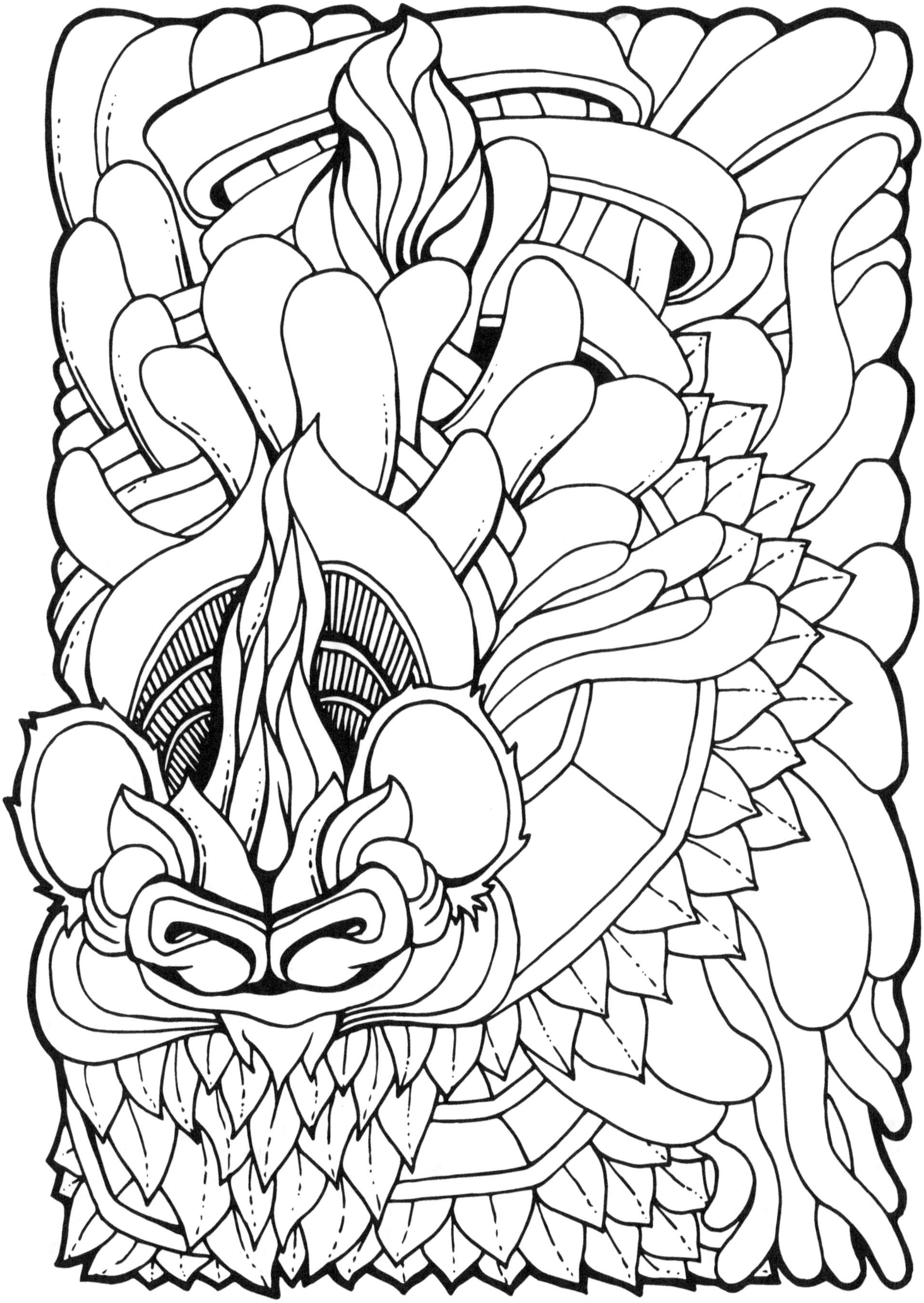

www.ingramcontent.com/pod-product-compliance
Lightning Source LLC
Chambersburg PA
CBHW081314170526
45166CB00011B/3523
9781519600196